CD INCLUDED

HAL•LEONARD
BIG BAND
PLAY-ALONG
VOLUME 7

PIANO

Standards

T0082974

ISBN 978-1-4234-5887-6

HAL•LEONARD®
CORPORATION
7777 W. BLUEMOUND RD. P.O. BOX 13819 MILWAUKEE, WI 53213

Visit Hal Leonard Online at
www.halleonard.com

AUTUMN LEAVES

English lyric by JOHNNY MERCER
French lyric by JACQUES PREVERT
Music by JOSEPH KOSMA
Arranged by PETER BLAIR

PIANO

From BORN TO DANCE

EASY TO LOVE
(YOU'D BE SO EASY TO LOVE)

Words and Music by COLE PORTER
Arranged by SAMMY NESTICO

Piano

GEORGIA ON MY MIND

Words by STUART GORRELL
Music by HOAGY CARMICHAEL
Arranged by MARK TAYLOR

PIANO

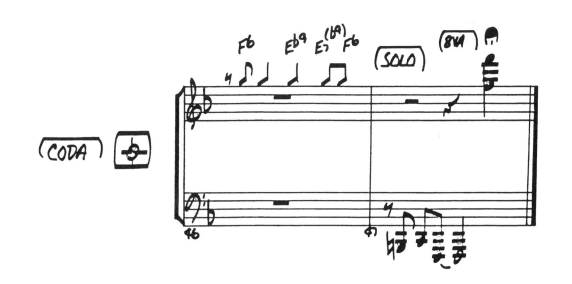

HARLEM NOCTURNE

Music by EARLE HAGEN
Arranged by JOHN BERRY

PIANO

14

THIS PAGE HAS BEEN LEFT BLANK TO ACCOMMODATE PAGE TURNS.

From STATE FAIR

IT MIGHT AS WELL BE SPRING

PIANO

Lyrics by OSCAR HAMMERSTEIN II
Music by RICHARD RODGERS
Arranged by MARK TAYLOR

JA-DA

Words and Music by
BOB CARLETON
Arranged by SAMMY NESTICO

PIANO

From BELLS ARE RINGING

JUST IN TIME

Words by BETTY COMDEN and ADOLPH GREEN
Music by JULE STYNE
Arranged by SAMMY NESTICO

Piano

From BABES IN ARMS
MY FUNNY VALENTINE

Words by LORENZ HART
Music by RICHARD RODGERS
Arranged by SAMMY NESTICO

Piano

From GOLDEN BOY

NIGHT SONG

Piano

Lyric by LEE ADAMS
Music by CHARLES STROUSE
Arranged by RICK STITZEL

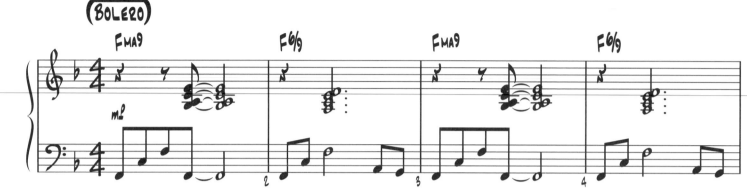

ON THE SUNNY SIDE OF THE STREET

PIANO

Lyric by DOROTHY FIELDS
Music by JIMMY McHUGH
Arranged by SAMMY NESTICO

Relaxed Jazz Feel (♩ = 104)

THE BIG BAND PLAY-ALONG SERIES

These revolutionary play-along packs are great products for those who want a big band sound to back up their instrument, without the pressure of playing solo. They're perfect for current players and for those former players who want to get back in the swing!

Each volume includes:

- Easy-to-read, authentic big band arrangements
- Professional recordings on CD of all the big band instruments, including the lead part
- Editions for alto sax, tenor sax, trumpet, trombone, guitar, piano, bass, and drums

1. SWING FAVORITES

April in Paris • I've Got You Under My Skin • In the Mood • It Don't Mean a Thing (If It Ain't Got That Swing) • Route 66 • Speak Low • Stompin' at the Savoy • Tangerine • This Can't Be Love • Until I Met You (Corner Pocket).

07011313 Alto Sax....................$14.95
07011314 Tenor Sax..................$14.95
07011315 Trumpet....................$14.95
07011316 Trombone..................$14.95
07011317 Guitar........................$14.95
07011318 Piano.........................$14.95
07011319 Bass...........................$14.95
07011320 Drums........................$14.95

2. POPULAR HITS

Ain't No Mountain High Enough • Brick House • Copacabana (At the Copa) • Evil Ways • I Heard It Through the Grapevine • On Broadway • Respect • Street Life • Yesterday • Zoot Suit Riot.

07011321 Alto Sax....................$14.95
07011322 Tenor Sax..................$14.95
07011323 Trumpet....................$14.95
07011324 Trombone..................$14.95
07011325 Guitar........................$14.95
07011326 Piano.........................$14.95
07011327 Bass...........................$14.95
07011328 Drums........................$14.95

3. DUKE ELLINGTON

Caravan • Chelsea Bridge • Cotton Tail • I'm Beginning to See the Light • I'm Just a Lucky So and So • In a Mellow Tone • In a Sentimental Mood • Mood Indigo • Satin Doll • Take the "A" Train.

00843086 Alto Sax....................$14.95
00843087 Tenor Sax..................$14.95
00843088 Trumpet....................$14.95
00843089 Trombone..................$14.95
00843090 Guitar........................$14.95
00843091 Piano.........................$14.95
00843092 Bass...........................$14.95
00843093 Drums........................$14.95

4. JAZZ CLASSICS

Bags' Groove • Blue 'N Boogie • Blue Train (Blue Trane) • Doxy • Four • Moten Swing • Oleo • Song for My Father • Stolen Moments • Straight No Chaser.

00843094 Alto Sax....................$14.95
00843095 Tenor Sax..................$14.95
00843096 Trumpet....................$14.95
00843097 Trombone..................$14.95
00843098 Guitar........................$14.95
00843099 Piano.........................$14.95
00843100 Bass...........................$14.95
00843101 Drums........................$14.95

5. CHRISTMAS FAVORITES

Baby, It's Cold Outside • The Christmas Song • Feliz Navidad • I'll Be Home for Christmas • Let It Snow! Let It Snow! Let It Snow! • Little Saint Nick • My Favorite Things • Silver Bells • This Christmas • White Christmas.

00843118 Alto Sax....................$14.95
00843119 Tenor Sax..................$14.95
00843120 Trumpet....................$14.95
00843121 Trombone..................$14.95
00843122 Guitar........................$14.95
00843123 Piano.........................$14.95
00843124 Bass...........................$14.95
00843125 Drums........................$14.95

6. LATIN

Água De Beber (Water to Drink) • At the Mambo Inn • Bésame Mucho (Kiss Me Much) • The Look of Love • Mambo No. 5 (A Little Bit of...) • Mas Que Nada • One Note Samba (Samba De Uma Nota So) • Quiet Nights of Quiet Stars (Corcovado) • Ran Kan Kan • St. Thomas.

00843126 Alto Sax....................$14.99
00843127 Tenor Sax..................$14.99
00843128 Trumpet....................$14.99
00843129 Trombone..................$14.99
00843130 Guitar........................$14.99
00843131 Piano.........................$14.99
00843132 Bass...........................$14.99
00843133 Drums........................$14.99

7. STANDARDS

Autumn Leaves • Easy to Love (You'd Be So Easy to Love) • Georgia on My Mind • Harlem Nocturne • It Might As Well Be Spring • Ja-Da • Just in Time • My Funny Valentine • Night Song • On the Sunny Side of the Street.

00843134 Alto Sax....................$14.99
00843135 Tenor Sax..................$14.99
00843136 Trumpet....................$14.99
00843137 Trombone..................$14.99
00843138 Guitar........................$14.99
00843139 Piano.........................$14.99
00843140 Bass...........................$14.99
00843141 Drums........................$14.99

FOR MORE INFORMATION,
SEE YOUR LOCAL MUSIC DEALER,
OR WRITE TO:

HAL•LEONARD® CORPORATION
7777 W. BLUEMOUND RD. P.O. BOX 13819
MILWAUKEE, WISCONSIN 53213

www.halleonard.com

Prices, contents, and availability subject to change without notice.

0509